NORMA[...] [...]er since receiving the [...] [...] Bruce as a youngster. He studied Scottish History at university, although little has been retained. He still doesn't know if James IV was a Renaissance Prince or not.

He has devised websites for the Scottish Government on Scottish history, including one on William Wallace. As a result, he spent far too long watching Mel Gibson's *Braveheart* for research.

In his spare time he has written comedy for radio, TV and books. His proudest comedy moment is making Radiohead singer Thom Yorke laugh out loud on Radio One.

After a spell writing non-fiction history books, he felt it was time to use his accumulated knowledge for more light-hearted ends.

If History Was Scottish is his sixth book.

By the same author

I See... Modern Britain (Portico 2008)
I See... Xmas (Portico 2008)
Chronologia: 24 Hours of History (The History Press, 2012)
The Glasgow Book of Days (The History Press, 2013)
The Little Book of Aviation (The History Press, 2013)

If
History
was
Scottish

NORMAN FERGUSON
with illustrations by
BOB DEWAR

Luath Press Limited
EDINBURGH
www.luath.co.uk

First published 2013

ISBN: 978-1-908373-67-0

The paper used in this book is recyclable. It is made
from low chlorine pulps produced in a low energy, low emissions manner
from renewable forests.

Printed and bound by
Martins the Printers, Berwick upon Tweed

Typeset in Quadraat and MetaPlus
by 3btype.com

M & D *for starting it all.*

Contents

Introduction

HISTORY IS FULL of powerful and colourful characters – those that grabbed their chance for immortality, lusting after their spot in the pantheon of the famed. There's Alexander the Great, Peter the Great, Catherine the Great, Frederick the Great, Otto the Great, Alfonso the Great, Hugh the Great, and Alfred the Great. None of whom are Scottish. There is nothing a Scot could do to earn that level of nomenclaturive praise: Alexander the Awright, Peter the Okay, Catherine the No' Bad maybe.

As we know, Scotland has produced numerous figures of note but none of them are suffixed 'the Great'. Even King Robert I whose tireless efforts freed a country from under the yoke of oppression only gets 'the Bruce', which is his surname.

However, this book isn't about him or any of those from his country, it's about the other world – the non-Scottish world – but seen as if infused with the qualities that make up a collected form of Scottishness: the caustic wit, the shrewdness, the ultra-cautiousness, the sentimentality, the pride and the ease of issuing judgment, to name but a few.

Welcome to an alternative world, where all history is Scottish.

Norman Ferguson
2013

'Ah wiz there'
Forrest McGump

'And God looked upon
the world he had created.
And it wasnae bad.'
Bible

Afore-History

'It's cauld enough for snow.'
Ice Age

– 'Ug ug raaar ug!'
– 'Yer jist showing off now.'

'Playing Pictionary in these caves is nae use,
you can hardly see. Is that a deer? A cow?
A dug?'
Lascaux, France

'So this wheel thing, is it expensive?'

Biblical Times

'We'll get the tatties in there, then carrots and neeps over there.'
Adam and Eve, Garden of Eden

'Old age doesnae come itself.'
Methuselah

'Thought this was a square go? Whit's with the catapult?'
Goliath

'Pretty nice jacket, eh? Slater's sale, half price.'
Joseph

'Right lads, this ark will be built at this yard. So there will be no hooliganism, no vandalism and no bevvying.'
Noah

IF HISTORY WAS SCOTTISH

'Forty days and nights of rain? So what,
I'm from Fort William.'
Noah

'Foo's yer doo's?'
Noah's wife

'Did I hear right, there's free tablet going?'
Moses

'Hame'll dae us.'
Moses

'Here, you'll want to see this,
it's my new party piece.'
Moses, Red Sea

'This place is hoaching with locusts.'

'Just a trim thanks, leave a bit on
the lugs.'
Samson

'That noise would give your erse
a sare heid.'
Jericho

The Ten Commandments

Nae worshipping other deities
Nae making models of anything and then
    worshipping them
Nae saying Jeezo, Crivens, et cetera
Nae doing anything on Sundays
Keep in with yer maw and paw
Nae offing people
Nae footering aboot with other folk
Nae knocking stuff
Nae making up clipes
Nae fancying others' gear

'We have brought gifts: gold,
frankincense and mair stuff
we've left on the camel.'
Three Wise Men, Bethlehem

'Excuse me, Jesus, would you mind
closing the door? Were you born in a barn?'
Nazareth

'Thon Jesus thinks he's something.
I kent his faither.'
The Mount

'40 days in the wilderness?
He should try driving through Livingston.'

'Careful, Lazarus, you're a long time deid.'

'Just so I'm clear, we need:
5,000 single fish – with buttered bread.'
Jesus, Bethsaida

'Judas is hingin' aboot like a reek of gas.'
Garden of Gethsemane

Ancient

'Oh we had awfy trouble with our polis too.
They ate all wur doughnuts and never solved a
single crime.'
Greece

'So we've only got ane set of goalposts
and the pitch is circular? Well done, numpties.'
Stonehenge

'All hail sun god Radge.'
Egypt

'Build them just like the teabags.
No, not they circular ones, the pyramiddy ones.'
Imhotep

'What did your last slave die of?'
Building of the pyramids, Giza

'Make sure all this goes in the vault with me
– I don't want any in cash converters.'
Tutankhamun

'I'm no complaining. It's steady work.'
Sisyphus

'Wait 'til your faither hears about this.'
Oedipus' Mother

'Dinnae be daft; the sun's no' hot
enough to melt wax.'
Icarus

'So you want me to build a horse able to hold a
squad of soldiers? Mmm, I could fit you in
mebbe next week? Gonnae cost you, mind.'
Troy

'We were raised by wolves but we're alright
noooooow!'
Romulus and Remus

'And Best in Bloom 600BC goes to... Babylon.'

'Oh magic, mair columns.'
Parthenon opening

'Death is no' tha worst that can happen to men.
Have you never eaten potted hough?'
Plato

'Hemlock. No' had that. Don't mind if I do.
Cheers!'
Socrates

'Alexander the Great? Wha does he think he is?
Alexander the No'-So-Bad maybe.'

'This knot is in a right fankle.
Hand me my dirk.'
Alexander the Great

'This coupon's launched a thousand ships
by the way.'
Helen of Troy

'You beauty!'
Archimedes

'Ride elephants over the Alps?
You been drinking?'
Hannibal

'Carthage's been sacked?
Was he a bad manager?'

'I came, I saw, I got conniched.'
Julius Caesar

'I'm no' Spartacus!'

'Emperor Caesar, may we present
the new Julian calendar for your approval.
The Scottie dog picture is awfy cute,
do you no' think?'
Rome, 44BC

'And you, Brutus.
I kent you'd be involved in this.'
Julius Caesar

'Installing my horse as consul
will bring stable government.
Do you geddit? It's good that.
Laugh or I'll chop yer heid off.'
Caligula

'I hope that's no' skimmed milk in this bath.'
Cleopatra

'She's all fur coat and no drawers.'
On Boudicca

'I ken the city's on fire,
but Robbie Shepherd's come a long way
and I'm not letting him away
before hearing my 'Hieland Laddie'.'
Nero

'I've just dusted that carpet too.'
Pompeii

'Wur doomed!'
Pompeii

'This wall's not to keep them out.
It's to keep my men from that
bloody awful diet.'
Hadrian

'That's the snakes gotten rid of.
Midgies? I'll get back to you.'
St Patrick

'We've done a monkey, a spider, whit's next?
Let's dae a flying saucer
– get them aw guessing.'
Nazca Desert, Peru

'That's Attila at the door.'
Thermopylae

IF HISTORY WAS SCOTTISH

'Wild horses wouldnae drag me to Abbeville.'
Brunhilda of Austrasia

'You'll no' be peeking o'er into
our garden much noo.'
Building of Great Wall of China

Peck away for all you like,
my liver's harder than a walnut.
Prometheus

Middlin' Ages

'Anybody want a well-fired cake?'
King Alfred

'Here, less of the 'Auld Yin'.'
Edward the Elder

'I'll get up and make the tea,
everyone stay where you are. It's fine.'
Edward the Martyr

'I'm coming. Haud on a minute!'
Ethelred the Unready

'Your heid will remain in the lavvy bowl unless You. Give. Me. Your. Dinner. Money.'
King Fruela the Cruel

'Whit's first base?'
King Alfonso the Chaste

'Yass. Found anither gold coin doon the sofa.'
Leif 'the Lucky' Eriksson

'My feet are fair giving me gyp.'
King Bermudo the Gouty

'That Eadric Streona is a
gigantic pain in the erse.'
King Edmund II

'Whit're you moaning aboot?
You've got another eye.'
Battle of Hastings

'Right whit's your name and whaur
dae ye bide?'
Domesday Book survey

'I don't care if it's my hen do,
I'm no' riding down the high street naked.'
Lady Godiva

'As if the exam for being king isn't
hard enough without having to pull a sword
oot o' a boulder.'
King Arthur

'No no, I'm almost there, I'll get this jar open
myself thanks.'
King Alfonso the Battler

'That's pure magic.'
Merlin

'Come ahead, ya big ocean!'
King Canute

'See, good as new.'
King Garcia Ramirez the Restorer

'I'm always late.'
King Theobold the Posthumous

'No I'm not, I'm jist big-boned.'
King Henry the Fat

'Ferdy! Come here when I shout on you.'
King Ferdinand IV the Summoned's mum

'Who can? Genghis Khan!
That's gonnae catch on I tell you.'
Genghis Khan

'No, you started it.'
King Louis the Quarreller

IF HISTORY WAS SCOTTISH

'Aye I like basketball. Aye it's handy for getting things from shelves. And aye the weather up here is great. Any mair daft questions?'
King Philip the Tall

'It's normal for a tower like that. It'll settle fine.'
Pisa

'You'll see my erse on that horse over my deid body.'
El Cid

'It wisnae me.'
Edward the Confessor

'Can I no' get peace from this turbulent priest?'
King Henry II

'It's roastin' the day.'
Joan of Arc

'Hello, chinas!'
Marco Polo

'There's nae hot water after 2.30pm.'
Kublai Khan's Xanadu

'I'm no' getting the bum's rush here I hope?'
Edward II

'There's a rat loose aboot this hoose.'
The Black Death

'This'll no' be over by Christmas.'
100 Years War

'So, Robin, what chippie does this Fryer Tuck work at?'
Little John

'I'm coming but I cannae stay up long.'
King Henry IV the Impotent

'Are we no there yet?'
Vasco De Gama

IF HISTORY WAS SCOTTISH

'At last my printing press is ready.
I shall begin... the People's Friend.'
Johannes Gutenberg

'People say I'm stuck up.
That couldnae be further frae the truth.'
Vlad the Impaler

'I don't have a scooby where we are.'
Henry the Navigator

'If I say it's India, and you say it's India,
and we all say it's India – then it's India, right?'
Christopher Columbus

1500s
Bags of Tudors

'Michelangelo, you've missed a bit.'
Pope Julius II, Sistine Chapel

'See Martin Luther and his Diet of Worms?
I might try it.
Got to shift a few pounds by our holidays.'

'Oh, Ivan, you're an awfy man.'
Russia

'I never thought the Prophecies
would sell so well.
Didnae see that coming.'
Nostradamus

'I'll get my revenge, you jist wait.'
Montezuma

'It's no skin aff ma nose.'
Tycho Brahe

'It's a braw, bricht, moonlicht nicht.'
Galileo

King Henry VIII:
'You have sent me a Flanders mare!'
Anne of Cleeves: 'And I've met a horse's erse.'

'He's no oil painting.'
Hans Holbein, on King Henry VIII

'Sixth time lucky?'
King Henry VIII

'She's a right nippy sweetie.'
On Mary Tudor

'In the country of the blind the one-eyed
man is on a good
disability pension.'
Erasmus

'I've got an empty –
who's up for a wee
party?'
Cesare Borgia

DUB

IF HISTORY WAS SCOTTISH

'Grumpy old besom is that Moany Lisa.'
Leonardo

'To God I speak Spanish,
to women Italian, to men French,
to my horse German,
and to my pub mates – pish.'
Emperor Charles V

'Listen, Martin Luther,
one mair toot and you're oot.'
Pope Leo X

'I want no peasant in my kingdom
so poor he is unable to have
chicken tikka masala every Sunday.'
King Henri IV

'Oh I'll be finishing my bowls first.
We've Port Glasgow next weekend
and they're no mugs.'
Francis Drake, Plymouth Hoe

'This brand new jacket?
Over a puddle? Get real.'
Walter Raleigh

'Where've ye been?
Whit time d'ye call this?'
Spanish Inquisition

'This job's pure murder at the moment.'
Tomas De Torquemada

'You bring me tatties and tobacco.
What use will my people have for these?'
Queen Elizabeth I

'This'll kill or cure me, that's for sure.'
Walter Raleigh on the scaffold

'Her Majesty Queen Bess
looks très peely-wally these days.'
Andre Hurault, French Ambassador

'No, I'm no in the huff.'
William the Silent

1600s
Uncivil Wars

'First things first: get the scouting party out on the search. There's got to be a pub round here somewhere.'
Pilgrim Fathers

'In the name of the wee man – go!'
Oliver Cromwell

'Your capes are all on shoogly nails.'
Oliver Cromwell

'I see the birds have shot the craw.'
King Charles I

'Awright, awright, keep the heid.'
King Charles I

'I think, therefore I am. I drink,
therefore I am your bezzy mate.'
Rene Descartes

'You wouldnae have a light on you would you?'
Guy Fawkes

'That Guy Fawkes is a lad o' pairts alright.
About five I think.'
Old Palace Yard, Westminster, 31 January 1606

'Dear Diary. Woke up, went out,
had ma dinner. Didn't get plague. Result.'
Samuel Pepys

'My latest work is entitled 'Paradise Lost'.
Original title: 'Dundee's Traffic System'.'
John Milton

'It's awfy fantoosh.'
Taj Mahal opening

'It's better than a slater up yer nose.'
The Man in the Iron Mask

IF HISTORY WAS SCOTTISH

**'Never mind your house,
the pies're burning!'**
Pie shop owner, London, 1666

'Haud yer wheesht!'
Christopher Wren,
opening of Whispering Gallery, St Paul's

'Guid gear comes in sma' bulk'
Tom Thumb

'I'm getting nowhere.'
John Bunyan

'Isaac, no one likes a smart arse.'
Publication of *Philosophiæ Naturalis Principia Mathematica*

'Well it's not Hamilton Palace but it'll do.'
Louis XIV, opening of Versailles

'We, the Pennsylvania Scots, will settle here and henceforth be known as The Hamish.'
Pennsylvania

So will I get time and a half
for working a public holiday?
Father Christmas

Shakespeare

'To be or not to be – what kind
of a stupid question's that?'
Hamlet

'My kingdom for a horse?
Think my head's buttoned up the back?'
Richard III

'Is this a chib I see before me?'
Macbeth

'Out out damned spot. Where's Molly Weir
when you need her?'
Lady Macbeth

'Dad, what a fleg you gave me there.
I thought you were deid.'
Hamlet

'Romeo, Romeo, where in Forfar art thou?'
Romeo and Juliet

'Cry havoc, and let slip the wally dugs of war.'
Julius Caesar

'Shall I compare thee to a Summer's day?'
– 'Sorry I need to stop you there.
Whit's a summer's day?'
Sonnet 18

1700s
Enlightening Times

'Let them eat Tunnock's Teacakes.'
Marie Antoinette

'Sit and deliver.'
Dick Turpin

'Shares in the South Sea Company,
two for a pound, two for a pound-ah!'

'Sorry darling, I'm going to have
to love you and leave you.'
Giacomo Casanova

'He's got a face like a well-skelped erse'.
On the Marquis de Sade

'Come on now, chop chop.'
Robespierre

Frederick the Great:
'Ya rascals, do you want to live forever?"
The troops:
'Aye.'

'I've been to other places, y'know.'
Clive of India

'I asked for a cuddle, not a cuddie.'
Catherine the Great

'This is as black as the Earl of Hell's waistcoat.'
Calcutta

Admiral:
'So, Captain Cook, we wish you to sail to the South Pacific and make observations of the forthcoming eclipse of the sun. What say you?'
Captain Cook:
'Well, it'll not observe itself.'

'It's tatties over the side.'
Boston harbour, 1773

**'The new taxonomic classification
system is as follows:
Birdies, Beasties, Floo'rs, Mannies
and Wifies, Creepy-crawlies.'**
Carl Linnaeus

**'So we're at war with America,
and I'm the mental one?'**
King George III

'Taps aff.'
The Sun King, King Louis XIV

'Je suis dans une droite etat.'
King Louis XIV

**'There is nothing certain in life
except death and taxes.
And Scotland being utter mince at football.'**
Benjamin Franklin

**'I cannot tell a lie. A big boy cut
that tree doon and ran away.'**
George Washington

'Ach away and fly a kite.'
Mrs Benjamin Franklin

'Who breaks into a prison?'
The Bastille, 1789

'Mr Christian, I'll see you later.
You can count on it.'
Captain Bligh, HMS *Bounty*

'Aye there's a wrongness there.'
On King George III

'I hereby claim this far-flung
land of Botany Bay.
We shall now compose a song
lamenting the distance from our homeland.'
Captain Cook, New South Wales, 1770

1800s
Mills and Looms

'Oh Josephine, gie's peace the night.'
Napoleon

'Scotland Expects... very little.'
Horatio Nelson, Trafalgar

'Och, dinnae be daft.
He'll never hit me from there.'
Horatio Nelson, Trafalgar

'We'll no' be back.'
Napoleon, retreat from Moscow

'Lord Byron? Mad bad and dangerous to know? I've another word: bampot.'

The Beaufort Scale

Scale	Description
Number One:	Nothing.
Number Two:	Hardly anything.
Number Three:	A tiny breeze.
Number Four:	Wee bit of a breeze.
Number Five:	Okay, a breeze.
Number Six:	Windy enough.
Number Seven:	Good drying weather.
Number Eight:	Bit blowy.
Number Nine:	Brolly reversing weather.
Number Ten:	Blowing like a gale.
Number Eleven:	A gale.
Number Twelve:	Bring the washing in.

IF HISTORY WAS SCOTTISH

'I've no idea the effect they have on the enemy but they give me the Squeaky Bum.'
Duke of Wellington

'Our army is composed of the scum of the Earth – the pure scum of the Earth so they are.'
Duke of Wellington

'I'll plant them here and in 30 years' time we'll have an abundance of... apple turnovers.'
Johnny Appleseed

'If an army marches on its stomach
my fattie-tatties are unstoppable.'
Napoleon

'Would the boats no' go faster
with an engine?'
First Oxford-Cambridge boat race

'See the slavery – gonnae no dae that?'
William Wilberforce

'C'mon and get aff.'
George Stephenson, Rainhill Trials

'My new novel is about the people of Kilmarnock.'
Victor Hugo

'So, Crapper, you reckon this 'toilet' of yours is revolutionary?
I hope you're no' yankin' my chain.'

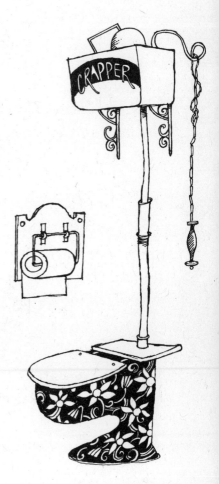

'Do you see me laughing?'
Queen Victoria

'I have made careful and
lengthy studies of the finch species
on this island and conclude that
they taste braw in a pie with mixed veg.'
Charles Darwin, Galápagos Islands

'That's a bobby dazzler.'
Koh-i-Noor diamond being presented
to Queen Victoria

The Charge of They Must Be Licht Brigade
Battle of Balaklava, Crimea

'God is pan breid.'
Nietzsche

**'Gonnae put that light out?
Folk trying to sleep here.'**
Florence Nightingale's Scutari Hospital, Crimea

'Grow up, will you?'
To William H Bonney aka 'Billy the Kid'

**'Don't even think of putting
'A Big' in front of my name.'**
Jesse James

'Where's the reinforcements?
Custer-Nae-Mates, that's me.'
General Custer

'Haud yer horses.'
Geronimo

'Awright, troops?'
General Ulysses S Grant

'Gettysburg? Get tae ****.'
General Robert E Lee

'You can fool all of the people
some of the time, you can fool
some of the people all of the time
and that's long enough to get
them to visit Saltcoats.'
Abraham Lincoln

'You plan a wee night out to the
theatre and there's always some
numpty who ruins it for everyone.'
Abraham Lincoln

'It's going like a fair today.'
Rorke's Drift

'This is awfy heavy.
Should have just made a bunnet.'
Ned Kelly

'You need your bumps felt
if you think this'll work.'
On Louis Braille's new invention

'I'm hardly going to cut off
my ear to spite my face.'
Vincent Van Gogh

'Wherever you be, let your wind gang free.'
Le Petomane

'From each according to his ability,
to each according to what he's wanting.'
Karl Marx

'History repeats itself, first as tragedy,
then as an episode of River City.'
Karl Marx

'War is hellish.'
General William Sherman

'Do you mind that Alamo?'

'Fools and bairns shouldn't
see a job half done.'
Antoni Gaudi

'Yoo hoo, anybody in?'
Discovery of the *Mary Celeste*

'Hello ladies. Yes, it's true,
I am gorgeous.'
King Ferdinand the Desired

'There's sillar in them thar hills.'
Klondike River

IF HISTORY WAS SCOTTISH

'We are still seeking clues as to
who this Jock the Ripper is.'
Police statement, Whitechapel, London 1888

'Gonnae stop ringing that
bloody bell and give me a biscuit?'
Pavlov's dog

'Doctor Livingstone? I thought it was you.'
Henry Stanley

'I have nothing to declare except my genius.
And two hundred Benson & Hedges.'
Oscar Wilde

Lie back and think of Scotland.
Victorian Marriage advice

**'You're no a better man than you
should be, Gunga Din.'**
Rudyard Kipling

'Roll up, roll up, anyone got a roll up?'
PT Barnum

**'Hurry up and get your finger out!
And in.'**
Haarlem Dyke, Netherlands

'Please, sir, gonnae gie's mair?'
Charles Dickens, *Oliver Twist*

'It was the worst of times,
it was the worst of times.'
Charles Dickens, *A Tale of Two Cities*

'It's not over 'til I sing.'
Queen Victoria

'You want seven and a half million
for Alaska? We'll wait for the sales.'
USA, 1867

IF HISTORY WAS SCOTTISH

'Why is the figure screaming?
You would too if you were in the Tartan Army.'
Edvard Munch

'I now declare the first modern
Olympic games open. The first event we have
today is...the tossing of the caber.'
Greece, 1896

'Despite what you've heard, I'm no deid.'
Mark Twain

1900s
The Bell Epoch

'I'm away to get the messages.'
Marconi

'This discovery of radiation will allow great advances in scientific applications. Chief amongst these is the ability to heat up a sausage roll in seconds flat.'
Marie Curie

Cycle round France? Is your car broken?
Inaugural Tour de France, 1903

'So someone walks in front of these
new-fangled motor cars with a red flag.'
'Ah right. Does that not make the car angry?'

'It got awfy shoogly. Then awfy burny.'
San Francisco, 1906

'Dib dib dib, dobber dobber dobber.'
Lord Baden-Powell

'I've come all this way, climbed all these hills
to find it's a bunch of ruins.
In a word – gutted.'
Hiram Bingham, Machu Picchu

'Wheeeeeeeee!'
Orville Wright

'E equals M C squared sausage.'
Albert Einstein

**'Genius is one per cent inspiration,
ninety-nine per cent sweaty oxters.'**
Thomas Edison

**'Can I stop you there?
Let's move onto the dirty bits first.'**
Sigmund Freud

IF HISTORY WAS SCOTTISH

'Here, careful handling the plane,
my duty free's in it.'
Louis Bleriot

'It's aw doonhill from here.'
Robert Peary, North Pole

1910s
Oh, What a Boggin' War

'The Belle Epoque? Oh we'll pay for this.'

'Women, children and bar staff first.'
RMS *Titanic*

'I'm just nipping out for a minute.
Anybody want anything from the shops?'
Captain Oates, South Pole

'It's just the sniffles.'
Typhoid Mary

'I don't think I can write much more.
Am absolutely jiggered.'
Scott of the Antarctic

'I don't care if they've shot
Belle and Sebastian in Selkirk High Street,
we're still not going to war over it!'
Prime Minister Asquith, Summer 1914

'That is bang out of order, by the way.'
Archduke Franz Ferdinand, Sarajevo, 1914

'It'll all be over by the tattie holidays.'
The Kaiser, 1914

'Game's a bogie.'
Western Front, Boxing Day, 1914

'You're no' here to enjoy yourself.'
Marshal Petain, Verdun, 1916

IF HISTORY WAS SCOTTISH

'Cludgie.'
Marcel Duchamp, 1917

'We're all Jock Tamsonovitch's bairns now.'
Lenin, 1917

'I have split the atom.
You would not believe how totie it is now.'
Ernest Rutherford

'My legacy will be a country's freedom.
And a moustache.'
Emiliano Zapata

'You can't shoot, poison,
throttle and drown a good man down.'
Rasputin

'We'll need to get shot of this Czar guy.'
Russia, 1917

1920s
The Roarin' and Greetin' Twenties

'Yes, bonnie things.'
Howard Carter, Luxor

'No mum, I've no' settled down, still courting.'
Rudolph Valentino

'God doesnae play dominoes.'
Albert Einstein.

'A verbal contract isn't worth
dichting your behind with.'
Sam Goldwyn

'Aye cheers, Stan, landing us in it again.
You're a right tube sometimes
did you know that?'
Oliver Hardy

'This is a painting of a pipe.'
Rene Magritte

'Ya dancer!'
Isadora Duncan

'I think the ladies will like my new creation: the little black joggy bottoms.'
Coco Chanel 1926

'Sorry mum but I am planning on treating this place like a hotel.'
Conrad Hilton

'I made him an offer he could refuse or accept. I left it totally up to him.'
Lucky Luciano

1930s
Flapping Thirties

'Yes, I know the eyes are squinty,
but it's art, awright.'
Pablo Picasso

'Why don't you come up and see me sometime?
Shoes off at the door, mind,
it's a new shagpile we've put in.'
Mae West

'I'll not be voting for that wee nyaff.'
Germany 1933

'Buddy, can you spare me
some spare change?'
USA, Depression

'Bugger Biggar!'
King George V

'That's their gas I'm peeping at.'
Herbert Morrison, *Hindenburg* disaster

'Is the cat dead? Mibbe aye,
mibbe naw.'
Erwin Schrödinger

IF HISTORY WAS SCOTTISH

The Big Deal
USA, 1933

'History is more or less keich.'
Henry Ford

'Get it right up you, Adolf!'
Jesse Owens, 1936 Berlin Olympics

**'You can have any colour you want –
as long as it's tartan.'**
Henry Ford

'Booze isn't being prohibited –
it is now compulsory.'
Volstead Act, USA

'This ground's dry as a badger's bahoochie.'
Dust bowl, USA

'I have evaluated my patients and conclude
that some are 'away mit der fairiesse'.
Carl Jung

CUPBOARD

'I am prepared for the worst, even death, in defiance of the Salt and Sauce Tax.'
Mahatma Gandhi

'Dream on.'
Carl Jung

'Well it's back to auld clathes and porridge.'
Edward VIII, on his Abdication

'Baggsy shotgun!'
Clyde Barrow

IF HISTORY WAS SCOTTISH

**'No it's not the Long Traipse,
it's the Long March.'**
Mao Zedong

**'The only thing we have to
fear is fear itself.
And being interviewed by Edi Stark.'**
President Franklin D Roosevelt

**'Of course aliens haven't landed
in New Jersey. Wise up.'**
Orson Welles

'I guess we're not in Kilsyth anymore, Toto.'
Dorothy, *The Wizard of Oz*

'Frankly, my dear, I'm nae bothered.'
Rhett Butler, *Gone with the Wind*

'I want to be on my Jack Jones.'
Greta Garbo

1940s
Mair War Years

'Who is it now? I need a visitor
like a hole in the heid.'
Leon Trotsky, Mexico

'Never in the field of human conflict
has so muckle been owed by
so monie to so mickle.'
Winston Churchill

'I can't make head nor tail of this code
malarkey. It's in a right guddle.'
Bletchley Park

'I don't want anyone hingin' around
that garage, right?'
Mussolini

'You'll have had your tea?'
Roswell, 1947

'The Buckfast stops here.'
Harry S Truman

'What a braw heat you get off that.'
Robert Oppenheimer, Manhattan Project

'Cheese!'
Henri Cartier-Bresson

'Here's to us, wha's like us?
 Everyone pretty much.'
UN Declaration of Human Rights, 1948

'We'll no' be making Irn Bru
from those girders.'
Tacoma Narrows Bridge collapse

1950s
The Cauld War

'Hey Tenzing,
I can see your house from here.'
Edmund Hillary, Mount Everest

'How can you govern a country which produces
265 different kinds of boiled sweet?'
Charles de Gaulle

The Skelp Heard Around the World
New York Giants stadium, 1951

'I'm singing, just singing, and going to work,
playing golf, taking the bins out,
washing the car, cutting the grass,
walking to the pub, posting letters,
buying a pint of milk, doing everything
– in the rain.'
Gene Kelly, 1951

'Don't be greetin' on my account.'
Eva 'Evita' Peron

I Don't Mind Ike
Pin badge, USA, 1952

'He's done it! Roger Bannister
has run the mile in under four minutes.
I don't know why, he's got a push-bike.'
Oxford, 1954

'Canal's aff.'
President Nasser, Suez

'You cannae shove yer granny aff this bus.'
Rosa Parks, Montgomery, Alabama

'Do not go gentle into that good night.
I'm pure raging, against the dying of the light.'
Dylan Thomas

Joseph McCarthy:
'Are you, or have you ever been, a member of the Communist Party?'
'Och son, I think you should keep your nose out other's affairs.'

'And now the new Queen emerges with the crown, sceptre and orb, and wearing the traditional ermine Paisley Shawl.'
Westminster Abbey, 1953

'Do you want fries with your chips?'
First McDonald's fast-food outlet

'It went straight aft agley.'
Bing Crosby

'If he keeps jiggling about like that,
the change'll fall oot his pocket.'
Elvis Presley appearance, Ed Sullivan Show

'Where the hell is he?'
Waiting for Godot

'Get aff your horse and drink your ginger.'
John Wayne

1960s
The Swingeing Sixties

'The wind of change is blawing through this continent.'
Harold MacMillan

'I didn't think getting a rocket at work would be like this.'
Francis Gary Powers

'There's not an awful lot up here.'
Yuri Gagarin

'Don't be asking what your
government can do for you,
put in a shift yourself.'
President John F Kennedy

'Gey close but no cigar.'
Fidel Castro to President John F Kennedy,
following Bay of Pigs invasion

'Happy Birthday, Mr President.
I've no' got you a present.'
Marilyn Monroe

'If you want me, thingummy, ring me.'
President John F Kennedy to Nikita Khrushchev,
Cuban Missile Crisis

'Ich bin ein Brechiner'
President John F Kennedy

'That clarty elephant's sharted on the flair.'
John Noakes, *Blue Peter*

Reporter:
'How did you find America?'
John Lennon:
'It's awright.'

'Look, Jack, what's for you won't go by you.'
Jackie Kennedy, Dallas, 22 November 1963

'I wish they all could be Killiecrankie girls.'
The Beach Boys

IF HISTORY WAS SCOTTISH

'And next on Top of the Pops it's Dave Dee,
Fan, Dabi, Dozi, Mick and Tich.'
Alan Freeman, 1966

'Turn On, Tune In, Get a Carry Out.'
Timothy Leary

'In the future everyone will appear
on the Fred Macaulay Show.'
Andy Warhol

'And the Russian's linesman's got his flag up.
No goal!
And the ref's sent Geoff Hurst off to boot!'
Kenneth Wolstenholme

'Naw.'
Charles de Gaulle, 1967

'Hey Brezhnev, get your tanks off my lawn.'
Alexander Dubcek, Czechoslovakia

'There's nothing easier gotten than a cheat'.
Doug Sanders, British Open, 1970

'I float like a butterfly and bite like a midgie.'
Muhammad Ali

IF HISTORY WAS SCOTTISH

'I am not the greatest.'
Muhammad Ali

'Let me reassure you, the pound in your pocket is still worth the same: hee haw.'
Harold Wilson

'Where's the burdz?'
Robert Stroud, Birdman of Alcatraz

'I'm going to save, save, save!'
Viv Nicholson

'Put it away, son. It's not big
and it's certainly not clever.'
The Doors concert, Miami, 1968

'5...4...3...2...1...Blast off.
We have lift off! Gaun yerself,
Apollo 11.'
Cape Kennedy, 16 July 1969

'That is a small step right enough.'
Neil Armstrong

'I have a dream, when folk from Glasgow and Edinburgh can sit on the same bus together in peace.'
Martin Luther King

'And if all your friends drove off the
pier would you do so too?'
Ted Kennedy's mother

'Excuse me while I punch this guy.'
Jimi Hendrix

1970s
Striking Years

'You're not going out like that
giving me a red face.'
Liberace's mum

'These'll fly off the garden centre shelves.'
Terracotta Army discovery, China

'That's shocking.
I can see the top of the lassie's semmit.'
Launch of Page 3

'We have coffee. Black or white.
Large or small. Take it or leave it.'
First Starbucks

'Fozzie, you muppet!'
Kermit the Frog

'Oh you are awful. No, really.'
Dick Emery

'You're lucky I'm in a good mood, punk.'
Dirty Harry

'He's minted but carries on as if
he doesn't have a pot to p**s in.'
On Howard Hughes

'I know it looks bad but
we'll get stock from the bones.'
Andes plane crash, 1972

Think Global, Go Loco.

'That was a sare fecht.'
George Foreman, The Rumble in the Jungle

'Houston, we have a problemo.'
Apollo 13

'I want to wake up in a city that never sleeps, even on half day closing on Wednesday.'
Frank Sinatra

'He was here one minute then away like snow aff a dyke.'
Lady Lucan

'Nobody can c u Jimmy.'
Jimmy Hoffa's disappearance

'Where there is discord, may we bring harmony.
Where there is error, may we bring truth.
Where there is doubt, may we bring faith.
And where there is despair, may we bring hope.
And if you believe that, you'll believe
    anything.'
Margaret Thatcher

FBI Most Wanted Cosy Nostra Members:

1   'Billy Big Lugs'
2   'Jimmy the Krankie'
3   'Tommy Two-Pints'
4   'Sammy Rickets'
5   'Joe Banana Fritters'
6   'Benny Small Rounds'
7   'Bobby Belly'
8   'Franky the Erse'
9   'Johnny Salt n Sauce'
10 'Don the Pie'

1980s
The Gimme Decade

'I'm not kissing the tarmac,
I dropped my pan drop.'
Pope John Paul II

'Lang may your lum not reek.'
Chernobyl

'Beat it, will you?'
Michael Jackson

'It's a monstrous plook on the face
of a much-loved and elegant friend.'
Prince Charles

'Sitties!'
Barbara Wodehouse

'What do we want?'
   – 'We're no' really sure.'
'When do we want it?'
   – 'Ach, whenever.'
Greenham Common, 1983

'You are joking, aren't you?'
John McEnroe

'And Smith won't score...
kent he wouldn't.'
Peter Jones, FA Cup Final 1983

'And Maradona rises with Shilton.
His hand is up. Oh it's in.
Perfectly good goal.'
World Cup 1986

'Chapping.'
Garry Kasparov

'Sláinte – where everybody
knows your name.'

'A woman telephoned earlier,
asking about a hurricane.
Well, aye, it's windy but there's
no need to get your bloomers in a twist.'
Michael Fish

'He thinks he's Erchie... Gemmill.'
On Maradona, World Cup 1986

'I think you'll find pedestrians
have right of way.'
Tiananmen Square, 1989

Advertising Slogans

I'd like to teach the world a few things.
Coca Cola

We'll take richt good care of you.
British Airways

I'd love a Babycham. Pint.

This train's taking an age.
British Railways

Whassup with your face?
Budweiser

It's good to sit still, in silence.
BT

Just dinnae do it.
Nike

IF HISTORY WAS SCOTTISH

For mash get a tattie masher.
Cadbury's Smash

Don't leave home with it in your wallet.
American Express

**Nothing comes between me
and my tracksuit.**
Calvin Klein Jeans

1990s
The Nineties

'Yer maw of all battles is underway.'
Saddam Hussein

'Mohammed was magic, a real stand-up guy.'
Salman Rushdie, *The Satanic Verses*

'It'll no' be you.'
National Lottery

'Make it so-so'
Captain Jean-Luc Picard, *Star Trek: The Next Generation*

**'If a midgie flaps its wings in Torridon,
does it start a hurricane in Peterhead?'**

**'I did not have rumpy-pumpy,
hanky-panky, nookie or how's yer faither
with that lassie, Miss Lewinsky.'**
President Bill Clinton

'When a trawler is followed by seagulls,
it gets covered in bird keich.'
Eric Cantona

'Have a no' bad day!'
America

2000s
The Jim Noughties

'There are kent kents.
These are things we ken that we ken.
There are kent unkents.
That is to say there are things
that we now ken we dinnae ken.
But there are also unkent unkents –
these are things we dinnae ken,
we dinnae ken. Ken?'
Donald Rumsfeld

'Please log into my new website:
Pusbook'
Mark Zuckenburg

'No, we cannae.'
Barack Obama

'Wee sleekit, cowerin,'
timorous dictator.'
US Army soldier, Tikrit, 13 December 2003

'It was tough down there.
But we've saved a fortune on pieces.'
San Jose copper mine, Chile

'I give to you our new product:
the AyePad.'
Steve Jobs

'I'll be down in a minute.'
Felix Baumgartner

Top 20 Pop Songs

1	Stairway to Leven	Led Zeppelin
2	Totie Dancer	Elton John
3	I'm Waiting for the Van	Velvet Underground
4	Total Myocardia of the Heart	Bonnie Tyler
5	A Whiter Shade of Peely Wally	10CC
6	Pretty Glaikit	Sex Pistols
7	These Boots are Made for Hill Walking	Nancy Sinatra
8	I Wanna Hold Your Drink	The Beatles
9	Uptown Ian Rankin	Althea and Donna
10	Sympathy for Dalziel	Rolling Stones
11	This Gormless Man	The Smiths
12	Motors	Gary Numan
13	Strathaven is a Place on Earth	Belinda Carlisle
14	One Night With The Bru	Elvis Presley
15	Is this the way to the Armadillo?	Tony Christie
16	Another One Bites the Crust	Queen
17	If You Wanna Be My Lumber	Spice Girls
18	Shake rattle and roll on butter	Elvis
19	I'm walking to New Cumnock	Fats Domino
20	Losing my Religious Bigotry	REM

20 Great Books
of Literature

Charles Dickens – *No Expectations*
DH Lawrence – *Lady Chatterley's Liver*
Alexander Solzhenitsyn –
   A Day in the Life of Ivan Doesnidaeashift
JRR Tolkien – *Lord of the Sovvy Rings*
Hubert Selby Jr – *Last Exit to Broxburn*
Ernest Hemingway – *The Sun Never Rises*
Khaled Hosseini – *The Kite Walker*
JRR Tolkien – *The Crabbit*
Milan Kundera – *The Unbearable Shiteness of Being*
John Steinbeck – *The Capes of Wrath*
Yann Martel – *Life of Pie*
Ian McEwan – *A tenement*
Audrey Niffenegger – *The Time Traveller's Bidie-In*
Amy Tan – *The Nae Luck Club*
Harper Lee – *To Fry a Mockingbird*
Charlotte Bronte – *Jane Ayr*
Salman Rushdie – *Midnight's Weans*
John le Carré – *Tinker, Tailor, Soldier, Clipe*
Jean-Paul Sartre – *The Boak*
Louise May Alcott – *Big Wummin*

Days of the Week:

Moanday
Bluesday
Wabbitday
Thirstday
Frieday
Swallyday
Soreday

Some other books published by **LUATH** PRESS

Haud ma Chips, Ah've Drapped the Wean!
Glesca Grannies' Sayings, Patter and Advice
Allan Morrison, illustrated by Bob Dewar
ISBN 978 1 908373 47 2 PBK £7.99

In yer face, cheeky, kindly, gallus, astute; that's a Glesca granny for you. Glesca grannies' communication is direct, warm, expressive, rich and often hilarious.

'Dinnae cross yer eyes. Ye'll end up like that squinty bridge.'

'Oor doctor couldnae cure a plouk oan a coo's erse.'

'This is me since yesterday.'

'That wan wid breastfeed her weans through the school railings.'

'Yer hair looks like straw hingin' oot a midden.'

'Ah'm jist twinty-wan an' ah wis born in nineteen-canteen.'

'The secret o' life is an aspirin a day, a wee dram, an' nae sex oan Sundays.'

Glesca grannies shoot from the mouth and get right to the point with their sayings, patter and advice. This book is your guide to the infallible wisdom of the Glesca granny.

Last Tram tae Auchenshuggle!

Allan Morrison, illustrated by Mitch Miller

ISBN 978-1-908373-04-5 PBK £7.99

Wur full! Everybuddy haud ontae a strap or yer man!

It's the end of the line for Glasgow's famous clippie, Big Aggie MacDonald, as her beloved trams are destined for the big depot in the sky.

Last Tram tae Auchenshuggle! is a trip down memory lane to 1962, with the Glasgow tram service about to come to an end. But Aggie wants to enjoy the last months on her beloved caurs, dishing out advice and patter with her razor-sharp wit to the unwary: the outspoken clippie who was never outspoken!

Big Aggie's tram is pure theatre, and the clippie is something else when it comes to dealing with fare dodgers, drunks, wee nyaffs, cheeky weans and high-falutin' wummen.

Get aff! O-f-f, aff! Dae ye no' undertaun' the Queen's English?

The historical realities of the Glasgow tramline are brought to life with Allan Morrison's hilarious patter. The last regular tram ran on 1 September 1962, and for the following three days a special service operated between Auchenshuggle and Anderston Cross. But even today the magic of the Glasgow trams has not been forgotten.

Bard fae thi Building Site

Mark Thomson

ISBN 978-1906307-14-1 PBK £7.99

Mark Thomson's powerful debut collection celebrates all things Dundonian; its people, its mills, its schemes, but above all its dialect. Writing solely in his 'mither tongue', Thomson demonstrates the flexibility of his native language in dealing with subjects from drug addiction to Scottish history to a man trying to chat up a woman. An intelligent discussion of working-class life, *Bard fae thi Buildin Site* is passionate and funny, tackling serious social issues as openly as love for one's family.

At last – a strang young voice fae Dundee.
MATTHEW FITT

[*Mark Thomson's poems*] *have a truth in them that comes directly off the page.*
TOM LEONARD

A book that doesn't pull any punches... working class poetry at its finest.

JACK McKEOWN, The Courier

Scots We Ken

Julie Davidson

ISBN 978-1-906307-00-4 HBK £9.99

Natives know them.
Visitors soon get to know them. Some, like the Golf Club Captain, the Last Publican and the Nippy Sweetie, are endangered species; others, like the Whisky Bore and the Munrobagger, are enduring figures on the Scottish landscape. Every generation produces its own variations on the Scottish character and it doesn't take long for the newcomers to become familiar social types like the MSP, the Yooni Yah, the Rural Commuter and the Celebrity Chieftain. Most Scots, if they're honest, will recognise a little bit of themselves in one or other of thes mischievous and frighteningly accurate portraits. Julie Davidson's wickedly observed profiles are complemented by Bob Dewar's witty drawings in this roguish gallery of *Scots We Ken*.

The Scots Julie Davidson kens is a triumph of canny Scots-watching. Here for the first time is the famous Davidson wry take on the foibles and pretensions of the sub-species Scotus Domesticus won from years of anthropological field work and now distilled into sharp witty draughts complemented by Bob Dewar's incisively drawn portraits.

MURRAY GRIGOR, Film-maker

Modren Scots Grammar: Wirkin wi Wirds
Christine Robinson
ISBN 978 1 908373 39 7 PBK £7.99

Good Scots is not bad English. But what is good Scots?

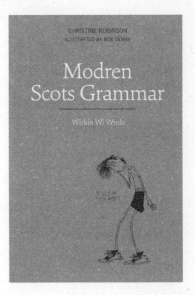

The Scots language is governed by grammar rules, just like any other language. In this book, you will find concise explanations, clear examples and exercises which allow you to practise what you've learned.

Topics covered include:

- Parts of Speech (nouns, verbs, adjectives etc.)
- Making sentences
- Phrases and Clauses
- Good style
- Punctuation

By the time you finish reading this book, you will have the tools needed to describe the Scots language correctly and confidently.

Luath Press Limited
committed to publishing well written books worth reading

LUATH PRESS takes its name from Robert Burns, whose little collie Luath (*Gael.,* swift or nimble) tripped up Jean Armour at a wedding and gave him the chance to speak to the woman who was to be his wife and the abiding love of his life. Burns called one of 'The Twa Dogs' Luath after Cuchullin's hunting dog in Ossian's *Fingal*. Luath Press was established in 1981 in the heart of Burns country, and now resides a few steps up the road from Burns' first lodgings on Edinburgh's Royal Mile.

Luath offers you distinctive writing with a hint of unexpected pleasures.

Most bookshops in the UK, the US, Canada, Australia, New Zealand and parts of Europe either carry our books in stock or can order them for you. To order direct from us, please send a £sterling cheque, postal order, international money order or your credit card details (number, address of cardholder and expiry date) to us at the address below. Please add post and packing as follows: UK – £1.00 per delivery address; overseas surface mail – £2.50 per delivery address; overseas airmail – £3.50 for the first book to each delivery address, plus £1.00 for each additional book by airmail to the same address. If your order is a gift, we will happily enclose your card or message at no extra charge.

ILLUSTRATION: IAN KELLAS

Luath Press Limited
543/2 Castlehill
The Royal Mile
Edinburgh EH1 2ND
Scotland

Telephone: 0131 225 4326 (24 hours)
Fax: 0131 225 4324
email: sales@luath.co.uk
Website: www.luath.co.uk